The

Enlightened Manager

Lessons on Leadership

by Michael Lisagor

The Enlightened Manager

Lessons on leadership

By Michael Lisagor

ISBN: 1438231016 and EAN-13: 9781438231013.

Published by: Custom Books Publishing

Order at: www.createspace.com or www.amazon.com

Printed in the United States of America.

Table of Contents

Introduction

Remember this also, and be well persuaded of its truth; the future is not in the hands of Fate, but ours.

—Jules Jusserand

At a banquet in Beijing in 1985, a seasoned Chinese government official told me the story of a tiny village in Hunan Province. Two young explorers had discovered a group of long-lost relatives 100 miles away. The elders ordered the construction of a road that would enable them to trade with the people in that town — a project that might take more than 50 years to complete. An impatient village youth exclaimed, "Why, that will take forever." One of the wise leaders replied, "Then we'd better start today."

One definition of enlightenment is hope. Another is the potential for wisdom and compassion that exists in each human being. Most people have some level of religious/spiritual conviction or moral compass, whether organized or not. So, why do so many managers leave this most important aspect of life at the door when they enter the workplace?

Many of the problems I encounter as a consultant stem from the inability of managers to perceive the world from an enlightened perspective. We can't always control what happens, but we often can control how we react.   Do we choose to respond to the daily challenges of management with anger and fear? Or can we learn to be compassionate and confident about the future?

An organization's growth depends on the vision of its leader and his or her willingness to change. Can we afford to neglect taking actions now that will ensure our organization's long-term success? Will our personality and good luck continue to drive our organization's growth? When do sound and humane business practices cease to be a luxury and become a necessity?

Do you grimace when someone mentions the word plan? Do you have one? If so, is it a living document that drives meaningful actions, or is it gathering dust on your office shelf? Are your subordinates comfortable telling you what they think, or are you as clueless as the emperor with no clothes? Will you always be a general of foot soldiers, or are you willing to become a general of generals? And perhaps most important, are you so consumed with achieving your objective that you've lost sight of your values? The answers to these questions will determine your organization's future.

This book is the result of more than 450 interviews I have conducted with industry and government executives and managers. It reflects the successes and failures of several businesses and government agencies -- some that are now large organizations -- others that have diminished in size and stature or disappeared altogether.

What compelled me to write this book more than anything was my belief that many of our business practices lack an underlying philosophical foundation. What is a manager's real purpose in life? Is it to amass as much wealth and recognition as possible? When did who we are become more important than how we behave?

I greatly appreciate: *Federal Computer Week* (1105 Media Inc.) for allowing me to develop the main messages of this book in my monthly *Enlightened Manager* column; my wife, Trude, for patiently reading everything I write; and Daisaku Ikeda for almost 40 years of spiritual encouragement.

Hopefully, what I've learned will stimulate your thinking, cause you to question a few of your sacred beliefs, encourage you to listen to your employees and to seek out the guidance of others.

Why bother? Because, while what you know will probably continue to contribute to your success -- what you ignore will most likely cause your failure and future unhappiness.

About the author

Michael Lisagor founded Celerity Works in 1999 to help executives accelerate business growth and manage risk. He also provides reality based risk management training and writes a management column for Federal Computer Week. Michael  has done over 450 organizational assessment interviews for over sixty government, industry and non-profit organizations.

Michael has an MS in management and has taught undergraduate marketing and project management workshops. He is the author of *Romancing the Buddha* (Middleway Press) and performs a one-man play based on this book (video available at amazon.com). Michael is also a popular motivational speaker. He lives with his wife, Trude, on Bainbridge Island, Washington, and can be reached at:

lisagor@celerityworks.com

206-780-4202 (PST)

Missing your mission

We all occasionally need a call to action

I recently rediscovered my sense of mission. It had disappeared without me noticing about a month ago. One day I was excited about my life — consulting, photography and writing — and then poof! Lights out! I suppose I could blame it on the holiday season. But that seems too convenient. My son-in-law gave me the book *The Radical Leap*, by Steve Farber, that reminded me of the importance of asking why I do the things I do. The gift was timely because I am helping a small technology company uncover its real objective so it can overcome its current organizational malaise.

I suspect many managers can relate to going through the motions at work without a feeling of enthusiasm for the task at hand. That attitude can result from a lack of direction, ineffective senior managers, interpersonal conflicts and a host of other factors. However, ultimately we have to be responsible for keeping track of our purpose. Managers must first reinvigorate themselves before they can inspire others.

So I put together a new mission statement, a call to action for myself. I started by answering several questions: What do I do? Whom do I do it for? Why do I do it? What impossible things could I make possible if I wasn't afraid of failing?

And just to make sure I did not lose sight of the big picture, I added, "What is my purpose in life?"

I recognize that some people might find this approach a bit esoteric. They might ask, "What difference does committing to a mission make if what you do is maintain networks, manage information technology contracts or review documents?"

But I have found that, to a large degree, my ability to maintain a lasting inner sense of purpose depends on my willingness to relate to an objective greater than my own immediate needs.

Such goals might be as simple as deciding to treat everyone with respect or as broad as ensuring that everyone in an organization communicates vital information quickly so they can fulfill their agency's mission or company's objective.

Enlightened managers not only recognize when they've lost their passion, they do whatever it takes to rediscover it and share their resolution with others. They recognize that the alternative is not acceptable.

Five habits of *incompetent* managers

No manager is an island!

I have a strong aversion to chain emails. Especially the ones that say I'll sprout something terrible like a second head unless I forward the message to ten of my friends. Still, I urge you to send a copy of this chapter to ten of your neediest co-workers; it may be their only hope! As for the head thing – no promises!

Based on numerous interviews, my own experience and an over stimulated imagination, here are five habits of highly *incompetent* managers and how to deal with these individuals.

Avoids making decisions. There is a time to self-reflect and gather information. There is also a time to fish or cut bait. This individual's inability to reach a timely conclusion drives you crazy and contributes to organizational malaise. Not unusual for this type of manager to avoid putting anything in writing. So, you should document any verbal direction and email it back to them for verification.

Treats staff like personal servants. Stuck in a bygone era, these managers have an over inflated sense of importance and a lack of respect for subordinates. Their style would work successfully on pirate ships but is not a motivating influence in modern organizations. Best to disconnect your phone to avoid their midnight phone calls and lock your office door to hide from late Friday assignments due on Monday morning. Better yet...move to another state.

Is too politically motivated. At the top of this individual's agenda is pleasing upper management. It comes before everything else including making the right decisions. Often collects facts only to ignore them or refuses to listen to bad news. Also has a difficult time staying on target or saying no to out of scope work. Avoids conflict by saying yes to everything instead of acting as a filter to prevent subordinate burnout. Deal with this manager by regularly presenting a list of your tasks and how many you can accomplish within your resource restraints. Wait for a prioritization or make your own.

Hides true project status. The bane of most complex projects, this program manager thinks risk avoidance means to only report the news that superiors want to hear. So, everything is always on schedule and within budget and everyone is happy – until everything and everyone isn't. Then it is time to blame others. The only cure, other than backbone implant elective surgery, is to carefully document the correct project status and keep on chugging.

Is technically proficient but people impaired. Beware technical experts with poor people skills. Rather than admit to a lack of management acumen, these managers accept ever increasing levels of responsibility without the necessary training. Their compensation and stature is inversely related to the number of subordinates who enjoy working for them. Agency and company heads too often look the other way figuring it's better to have a poor manager than none at all. These managers wallow in the details when they should concentrate on the bigger management issues. This will be a wonderful learning experience about how not to treat your staff when you get promoted.

Tone-deaf communications

The value of email depends

on how we use it

The Internet is truly a wonderful invention that allows us to communicate from a distance with large numbers of people. Our ability to share vital information and coordinate organizational activities is definitely enhanced. But once we enter the lively world of human emotions, watch out!

As a management consultant, I have experienced both the wonders and pitfalls of e-mail. Like most tools, its value depends primarily on how we use it.

Ever sent an angry response to an e-mail only to discover you misunderstood something and your emotional outburst was unwarranted? Wasn't it embarrassing? Could you have avoided some hurt feelings by calling instead?

Ever sent an innocent message only to have people respond angrily to something they misinterpreted?

According to researchers, seven percent of our communications is what we say, thirty-eight percent is the way we say it — rate, tone and inflection — and fifty-five percent is our body language before, during and after we say it. So, what we write to one another needs to be extremely concise to be correctly understood. E-mail is missing the crucial sounds of a human voice and the visual context clues that let us know what the sender is feeling and if the recipient is greatly upset, mildly peeved or encouraged.

In our rush to quickly share important information with as many people as possible, we often use e-mail as a shortcut. During the water-quality disaster caused by a hurricane that doused Washington, D.C., in 2003, information sharing was a lifesaver.

But when we're dealing with matters our co- workers feel strongly about, we are often too quick to hit the send button without adequate thought. It is very difficult to address someone's human nature through a computer.

It usually takes a person-to-person dialogue for us to be able to understand someone's true intention and avoid further aggravating a situation. This is how we can create harmony in our surroundings.

When I feel compelled to write an emotional e-mail, I send it to myself and reread it the next day before sending it on to others.

By taking time to reflect, I can ask myself why I don't just call the source of my frustration rather than sling a one-sided verbal arrow. Such arrows are impossible to recall and can cause considerable damage. In addition, I miss the opportunity to gauge the other person's reaction. How can I know if the recipient really understood what I meant if I can't see or at least talk to that person?

E-mail is great for communicating and clarifying simple schedule or meeting information and sharing policy guidelines. But if we're not careful, it can be a poor excuse for critical interaction. It takes our collective wisdom to use the full spectrum of human communication channels to build healthy organizations. So, the next time you have the urge to send some angry written words off into the World Wide Web, consider calling instead.

Breaking up is hard to do

Find ways to let go of poor

employees and bad habits

Letting go of things that no longer have value is difficult. In the personal realm, this includes dysfunctional relationships, unhealthy habits and, in my case, the compulsive need to make bad puns. For a manager, letting go takes on an even broader context because it affects not only your feelings, but also your organization's success and co-workers' performance.

An effective manager realizes that allowing someone to remain in a job that doesn't fit harms that person and the business. Many leaders are adverse to conflict and prefer to maintain a negative status quo rather than confront a performance issue directly.

But problems rarely go away without some intervention. You sometimes need to let go of staff members so they can find other job opportunities better suited to their skills.

Managers who were promoted from technical positions sometimes get mired in the details of a project, preferring to hide in the comfort zone of their previous responsibilities.

Managers who won't delegate tasks can cripple an organization. If you can't delegate, you will demoralize your employees and stall your career.

While you remain buried in minutiae, important management decisions go unattended. Letting go of less important technical details takes courage but is a sign of a mature manager.

People also get emotionally invested in certain design approaches, management solutions, technology projects and, in the case of industry, specific government business opportunities.

It can be difficult to separate enthusiasm, a positive trait, from an inability or unwillingness to objectively evaluate alternatives. If you're not careful, you can waste money on a losing proposition because you are unwilling to recognize a flawed plan.

When deciding whether to proceed with a plan or not, I like to use a decision matrix that requires the major stakeholders to assess the viability of an idea or project by scoring each critical success factor. If used properly, this approach can remove the raw emotions from the equation.

What is left is an objective view of whether the return on investment justifies the costs of workforce, IT infrastructure and financial resources.

People often avoid letting go because they fear uncertainty. But the act of moving on creates possibilities for something better. On the other side of uncertainty lies tremendous business and personal potential.

Enlightened managers are not afraid to take calculated risks. They accept that the status quo is not a friend to be trusted for too long. As the song goes, "breaking up is hard to do." But if you do, a new world of opportunities awaits you.

What they didn't teach me in school

Twelve lessons I wish someone

had shared with me

Meeting with university students is one of my most rewarding experiences. Their enthusiasm and desire to understand the "realities" of the professional world is infectious. To ease their post-college journey, I've developed twelve tools to take to work that I wish someone had shared with me when I was their age.

Don't feel entitled. The world doesn't owe us a living. The sooner we take the responsibility for our own success and happiness, the sooner we will switch from blame to taking action.

Establish meaningful relationships. Whether at school or at work, teamwork is often the key to project success. If you're on a ship, the fact that the hole is on the other side is little consolation.

Make a good first impression. We employ marketing techniques everyday with our families, friends and colleagues. We rarely make a poor first impression on someone on purpose. But, sometimes we forget to try. We try to present our value proposition in most meetings and, at some level, eventually we brand ourselves, hopefully with a positive identity.

Support your supervisor or leave. When we least want to talk to our boss is the most important time to knock on his or her door. It is the individuals we dislike that we can often learn the most from by engaging in honest, respectful dialogue. Don't run from adversity.

Respect others. Gossip and negativity create disunity, reflect poorly on our own character and drain our energy when we need it the most. There will always be something to complain about. So what?

Don't always have to be right. Co-workers who disagree with us aren't necessarily stupid. Other people usually want to succeed, too. Their values and perspective might just differ from ours. There isn't always a right and wrong way. Seek to understand other people's point of view and find win-win solutions.

Avoid negative behavior patterns. It is much easier to destroy than construct. Yet only construction results in positive results and personal growth and reward.

Expect difficulties. The environment reflects us – eventually we get what we need, but not necessarily what we always want and when we want it. Overcoming challenges is the door to personal and professional advancement.

Seek out a mentor. Those with more experience than us can help us find our way – help us navigate through the muddy waters. Most successful people have had one or more mentors.

Have hope. You can make a difference. Take pride in your abilities. One person can change the course of a class, a project or an entire nation. Seek out positive people when you're discouraged.

Concentrate on making a difference today. Each moment contains the past and the future. What is important is that we do our best today. That will set the course for the results we seek tomorrow.

Learn from our mistakes. And, also from the mistakes of others.

Innovation by listening

Listen to what your employees say

It was an endless late-night gathering. The doughnuts were stale. The coffee tasted like thick jet fuel. Discarded overhead transparencies, many never viewed, were scattered across a long mahogany conference table.

As a young department manager, I had just presented the truth about what I considered to be a foolish investment for company officials to make. Rather than trying to understand my rationale, my boss was shocked that I had the nerve to question his decision. I mentally collapsed in the corner — my career thoroughly riddled with verbal bullets. A few of my peers considered speaking up. "Wait!" they wanted to say. "There are major problems that still haven't been discussed." But they kept their own counsel. The fluorescent lights appeared to dim as the executive leaned back in his chair and told me to proceed with the ill-fated project.

Most of us have suffered managers who used their organizational mandate as an excuse to be impatient with dissenting views. It doesn't take long before staff meetings become rubber stamps for such an executive's decisions.

Many managers are so busy being busy that they barely have time to listen. Or they think that allowing their subordinates to speak out is a sign of weakness.

I once received feedback that my employees were upset when I answered my phone during conversations with them. They saw this as a clear indication that I didn't respect them or their time. So, I learned to let my voice mail answer the calls, or I started a meeting by explaining that I was expecting an important call. What really matters in life — our relationships with people — takes time to nurture and maintain.

It is vitally important to listen to what your employees have to say. They can provide insights that help you demonstrate appreciation for their contributions and experience and avoid critical mistakes. Unfortunately, organizations regularly promote otherwise talented managers who have the interpersonal skills of hyenas. This weakness often results in the inability to consider ideas that differ from their own, which stifles creativity.

Organizations eventually suffer from stagnation, degraded service and reduced profitability.

In my imagination, a young manager presents a contrary view at a late-night meeting. His supervisor welcomes the thorough analysis and praises his willingness to express reservations. The resulting dialogue leads to the implementation of some key risk mitigation measures. Promotions and bonuses are had by all!

Organizational growth requires both innovation and change. This can't take place if new ideas are suppressed. As managers, we need to engage in constructive conversations with our employees. The problems they reveal and insights they share are critical to long-term success.

New kids on the block

Realistic expectations can

prevent transition failure

I have worked for and managed many individuals who migrated from government to industry or from one type of industry to another. Their transitions have not always been smooth.

Some of the most painful experiences involved executives who were immediately placed in central leadership roles by their new employers. The employers assumed a seasoned manager from one type of business should be able to immediately manage a new culture. It was an unfortunate assumption.

I have distinct memories of one fresh-out-of-the-Army general who spent the first six months in shock when none of his staff responded to his forceful orders. Accustomed to relying on a cadre of junior officers, he didn't adjust to the minimal corporate overhead structure. Eventually, he was moved to a new program development corporate staff position in which he flourished.

Some individuals make the transition quickly. But for many, there is an adjustment period and expectations must be realistic so that the new employee isn't set up to fail.

Retirees must carefully define their values to a prospective employer. Industry officials are always on the lookout for government information technology managers with strong ties to agency decision-makers. New entrants into the commercial sector, however, should ensure that their new positions will allow them to exercise their management strengths, not just their contacts. Management skills are more enduring than rapidly changing agency organizational charts.

Some people might consider taking the consulting route if they are comfortable with sales and can legally engage in marketing activities.

Every organization has a unique culture. New employees, regardless of where they came from, would do well to ask probing questions about their prospective employers. How do they do business? Do they respect ex-government managers for their considerable prior experience? Do they value team players or independent producers? Do they provide broad technical and administrative support or expect each manager to stand alone? Are they family-friendly or do they expect employees to work long hours? What are the consequences of failing to produce expected results? Does the organization have a collaborative environment or a dictatorial hierarchy? Do the managers even know the difference? Join an organization without diligently asking such questions at your own risk.

In the final analysis, most managers find that they have a place in the new industry. Their first employer is often an experiment, but eventually they make their mark as dedicated and talented professionals.

Seizing the future

It's not just about the technology!

It seems to me that most senior executives have embraced the benefits of e-government and e-business. So, if the primary energy source of government improvement is electronic, what is our role? Could the missing transformational element in many organizations be you and me? Were we important all along but just didn't realize it?

During a speech at the *Building a Culture of Peace for the Children of the World* exhibit in the Rayburn House Office Building, Rep. Sheila Jackson Lee (D-Texas) encouraged staffers to be more than just members of a group but instead to live and work with a sense of mission. When I heard this, I couldn't help but reflect on how relevant this was to the role of a manager in government or industry.

Real leaders, I have been taught, should play to win and not just to finish. Yet how many workers put in the minimum required effort with the expectation that life doesn't begin until they leave work? How much richer would our lives be if we worked together with a sense of mission, a realization that what we do each day makes a difference in the world and to the future?

If we don't transcend technology with a strong sense of purpose, who will? We each have a choice. We can reluctantly work on tax modernization or fingerprint identification or Internet portals with the feeling that we are just another cog in a technology wheel.

But what would happen if even one manager became determined to create harmony on a project team? If he or she saw the positive potential in each team member? Helped someone uncover her unique contribution to system success? Replaced blame and judgment with hope and initiative? Chose a mission that went beyond just financial or career advancement?

We're all born members of one giant club: the human race. Eventually, we find ourselves constituents of many other smaller groups. The most important choice we make every morning is whether we transcend being passive members and rise up and take leadership roles. We've learned that technology by itself can't make the world a better place. But committed managers can.

This means not giving up when faced with seemingly insurmountable obstacles. Budget reductions, abusive bosses, organizational bureaucracy -- all these things can easily reduce us to blithering masses of emotional jelly. So what can we latch onto in these dark moments?

Representative Lee had it right -- it's the realization that we have a mission in this world. Our children are counting on us to get it right. Let's give we-government and we-industry a chance. It may be our only hope.

How to succeed in business

A leader needs to commit

to clear, measurable objectives

There is a common thread that runs through the business growth assessment interviews I perform. Managers often complain about conflicting and changing priorities, vague targets and unpredictable results, unsound investment strategies, unclear lines of authority and responsibility, management confusion and staff frustration.

Too many leaders echo Lily Tomlin's lament: "I always wanted to be somebody, but I should have been more specific."

An effective business plan describes an organization's focus — its mission, vision and objectives — in terms that are easy to understand.   There are myriad articles and books about how to write a business plan.

But the real challenge — what separates the slow-growth organizations from the barnstormers — is a leader's willingness to develop a business strategy that consists of clear and measurable objectives, has the support of key staff and is used throughout the year to measure progress and make decisions.

The age of omnipotent business leaders is over. And although this management model may produce near-term results, eventually even the most loyal subjects will rebel.

Unfortunately, a lot of managers still haven't learned that input from employees is crucial to successfully identifying the internal factors that will affect the organization's ability to sustain reasonable growth. And external changes in enabling technologies, budget and policy, market/citizen demand, competitor strategies and resource supply also need to be reflected in the business plan.

Business leaders who run their own strategic planning meetings are not always open to suggestions from staff about different strategies. How willing are employees to express their true opinions, especially in an open forum? A strong facilitator can usually level the playing field enough to allow an honest exchange of ideas, but even the world's most enlightened facilitator won't succeed if the leader resists change.

Incentive plans should reward behaviors and results that are consistent with strategic objectives. But strategic plans alone don't guarantee business growth — action plans do.

Strategic objectives must be translated into relevant and measurable actions assigned to individuals who are held accountable. Similarly, strategic actions should be monitored. If you don't care enough to ask your staff for a status report, they won't care enough to perform.

Finally, prioritize and estimate the cost and return on investment of each action. Then match all the actions with the operating budget. Only implement what is affordable. I've worked with several organizations that have developed a gigantic list of actions only to turn them over to managers for implementation in their spare time. This almost never works.

If I hear one more business manager declare, "We need to get it done with sweat equity," I'm going to scream! Aligning your investments with what you are talking about takes courage. But it's the only reliable way to become somebody. Just ask Lily.

Change starts at home

Old habits are difficult to break

Managing any kind of organization is a tough job. Even as a one-person consulting company, I face new challenges all the time. So it should come as no surprise that larger organizations often encounter significant barriers to growth.

Overcoming these difficulties requires a certain degree of cultural change. The willingness of leaders to alter their perspectives and behaviors is paramount.

Furthermore, a reluctance or inability to embrace the need for change will usually lead to stagnation. All the Program Management Institute knowledge in the world won't make up for a refusal to adapt.

The decision to propel an organization forward is usually met with the typical programmatic challenges and some resistance. Success requires management attitude and behavior changes.

Well, that's obvious, you might say.

My response would be to point out how often in my consulting work I encounter the ostrich syndrome. Have you ever left a meeting only to shake your head in disgust at some senior manager with his head in the sand who is unwilling to make a change that everyone else in the room knows is necessary? Now, be honest. Have you ever been that manager?

Any individual in an organization can make a difference. But, in general, the companies or agencies I've seen really take off — the ones I wouldn't mind my daughters working for — have had a leader who was willing to look in the mirror and lead by example. The leader would be willing to work on that one weakness that was preventing staff members from realizing their full potentials.

So, if your tendency is to micromanage, instead delegate some of the power and responsibility. If you're indecisive, make decisions in a timely manner. If you talk too much, listen more. If you blame others for what's wrong, be the change agent you want to see instead.

Old habits are difficult to break. I worked with one company executive who insisted on doing the detailed office assignments for the entire staff during a major facility move.

While he doodled on blueprints, business revenue tumbled. And his senior management team became so frustrated that some of them jumped ship.

You can't do the same things as a general that you did as a private. Yet one of the most difficult transitions at all levels of management is to let go of the details. It takes courage to entrust daily operations to others. This is especially tough for a manager who has moved up through the ranks of the technology staff.

But, unless you make this shift, your organization will almost definitely hit a wall. Or, as Benjamin Franklin said, "When you're finished changing, you're finished."

Controlling expectations

Learn how to say no

In 2001, I met with 25 industry project managers to share lessons learned and techniques to set, monitor, manage and reset client expectations and increase the probability of successful project implementation. Many of the suggestions also apply to government project managers.

Among the tips were:

1. Identify your stakeholders. Who has a vested interest in your project? Who has resources you need or will ultimately approve your project? Make sure you build a good rapport with these people.

2. Establish success criteria. You and your client should agree on what constitutes project completion. If you don't

achieve this understanding, you may never finish the project. Criteria are especially important on fixed-price deliverable tasks.

3. Get a solid start. Conduct thorough kickoff meetings and carefully document objectives, milestones and client responsibilities.

4. Review project status. Maintain a project plan. Review it weekly or biweekly with your team and the client.

5. Know your contract. Refer back to it before agreeing to additional tasks. You are responsible for controlling the scope of work and changes to it. Ignore the contract at your peril!

6. Be careful what you promise. Be willing to say no — nicely, at first, and more strongly when necessary — either when something your client wants is not in the baseline requirements or statement of work or when a request is unreasonable or unethical. Furthermore, you want to say no when it is something that would not be in the client's best interest. In such a case, you can say, "Our experience tells us that." But when you must say no, try to offer a more attractive alternative that solves the client's problem.

7. Actively seek feedback. Be willing to listen to your team members and client regarding what is and isn't going well. You can't fix a problem if you don't know about it. The issue you ignore or refuse to hear about could surface at a later date to torpedo your project.

8. Avoid surprises. When you discover potential problems with the project — such as risks and limitations — that may affect the outcome, develop contingency plans.

9. Communicate regularly. Recognize the major client relation danger signs. These include a lack of regular communication between you and your client; fear of talking to your client about something specific or, even worse, about anything at all; or uncertainty about your client's approval of what you are going to deliver.

10. Be proactive. Get your project out of trouble by listening to clients and understanding their concerns. You also need to bring an executive when you need to demonstrate commitment or when you have bad news. Finally, be honest: It's easier to remember the truth you told a month ago than the lie you told yesterday.

Relating to others

The importance of meaningful,

respectful dialogue

I have been making a concerted effort the past few years to accept my life as it is, both good and bad, instead of obsessing about how I wish it would be.

In the past, I spent considerable energy trying to reach an elusive "there," meaning everything is "good" — a promotion, a successful software delivery, a more pleasant boss or a little more money. It was almost impossible to enjoy my life when I was so busy waiting for something better to happen.

Speaking of elusive, I have also tried to work on how I relate to other people, especially business associates who give me grief. Many people I know have a tendency to label a manager who does something "bad" as being a bad person or something even harsher.

But as long as we judge others to the extreme, expecting them to behave perfectly, there will never really be an effective organization, much less a more peaceful world.

When I get upset with someone for something they have done or said, I try to reflect on that specific behavior instead of declaring the individual a lost cause.

By awakening my compassion for that person as a fellow human, I am able to communicate my concern without going into attack mode. It often means getting to know someone at a deeper level than the size of their office or how they behave during meetings.

This approach was very effective with one of my clients. Her demanding management style was preventing her staff from feeling free to express their opinions. In meetings, they would fight over who got to sit at the end of the conference table farthest from her and her verbal barbs.

Finally, when her behavior started to upset me, too, I realized I needed to talk to her. First, I accepted that her behavior was the problem, not her as a person. I also accepted that I could lose a valuable client as a result of broaching this subject with her. But I decided that it was more important to try to speak out against what I perceived to be unacceptable behavior than to swallow the pain out of fear of retribution.

After I had an honest discussion with her, she actually thanked me for pointing out why her actions were inconsistent with her desired company culture. And instead of canceling my contract, the next day she invited my wife and me to dinner.

This breakthrough was made possible only by transforming my initial negative, general judgment into a meaningful and respectful dialogue.

I try to remember that everyone has a unique contribution to make. This increases my appreciation of family, friends, associates and myself.

As an added benefit, my happiness today doesn't have to depend on some elusive tomorrow.

Organizational tapestry

Share information in an

open and collegial manner

New management levels complicate communications and often create personal fiefdoms with managers who have a vested interest in self-preservation.

Individuals filter and distort facts either unintentionally or by design. Top-down bureaucracies prevent the sharing of critical information. Faced with these seemingly insurmountable barriers to effective communication, what is an enlightened manager to do?

I recently attended a local city council meeting during which the level of arrogance and self-interest was mind-boggling. Council members did not appear to have a shared vision, sense of loyalty to associates or willingness to compromise. If this lack of coordination exists in such a relatively basic organizational structure, the difficulty in maintaining open channels of communication at large companies or government agencies is no surprise.

Flourishing organizations that achieve their objectives and respect their employees usually have enlightened leaders.

The need for managers to effectively communicate with those around them has never been more pressing. The rapid growth of technology has increased work complexity and the need to coordinate with many individuals located in multiple places and organizational units.

Unfortunately, managers' ability to share information in an open and collegial manner has lagged far behind the needs of modern organizations.

I think there is an underlying organizational structure or informal network that should embrace the official organization chart. It is like a tapestry that ties managers together with a common purpose. The organizational culture needs to promote this behavior.

Enlightened managers expedite and enhance the flow of information across these invisible threads. They filter out the minutiae and quickly forward necessary data. They avoid allowing biases and empire building to slow organizational growth. Becoming a better manager often means becoming a better human being. It means not allowing fear to dictate our behavior.

I'm afraid the hands we once used to lift the phone and the feet that carried us down the hall to clear up confusion or apologize have now atrophied.

The ability to listen is not a luxury. Treating employees with respect and compassion isn't just New Age mumbo jumbo.

Every manager can make a difference, and the more enlightened the manager is, the more enlightened the organization will be.

One small step

Learning from each other

I recently had the opportunity to ask 100 government managers to address the top information technology project management issues. The resulting discussions, while perhaps not earthshaking, were definitely one small step toward more successful projects of almost any variety.

Here are some of the observations they shared:

1. Identify responsibilities. They vary depending on the nature of the project. Taking the time to define a project's starting point is necessary for measuring progress and success. A well-defined baseline can be used to assign responsibilities, manage expectations, help resolve differences among stakeholders and overcome organizational barriers. Then you can share

project details with individuals based on their responsibilities.

2. Involve employees early when analyzing alternatives, so they will have a stake in the final product. Use prototypes or a statement of objectives — the project's vendor can help with the latter. Consider the larger business processes. Focus on significant process gaps.

3. Establish and integrate IT governance processes into projects and plan to measure their performance.

4. Communicate honestly with all employees involved in the project. Make communications a critical success factor for every program.

5. Develop a formal plan for managing risks. Clearly define requirements. But don't share risk management templates with stakeholders until you can explain how to apply them and know how to manage expectations.

6. Use the business case process to aid in starting and managing your project, not just as a paper exercise. When making decisions, ask: What is the value of doing the project? What is the impact of not doing it?

7. Appreciate the importance of earned value management. Past performance, cost and schedule data can be hard to access or lacking. Managers have been slow to develop the ability to measure performance on many projects, but it is a skill worth cultivating.

8. Have project managers shadow more senior program managers and participate in developing the business

case for an entire program. Support creation of a career path for agency project managers. Also, update the job series to allow for a clear distinction between project and program managers.

Old dogs, new tricks

Enlightened managers are open to change

Many people believe that you can't teach old dogs new tricks. But I disagree. As proof, I cite my work on this chapter. After reading the first draft, my wife calmly told me it needed a rewrite. I took several deep breaths, then accepted her critique with gratitude instead of anger — and avoided landing in the doghouse.

Few people enjoy receiving criticism, constructive or otherwise. But reluctance to change can cause even more problems. Bad habits left unchecked often become major management stumbling blocks.

During a behavior simulation feedback session, an irate manager told me that my sense of humor had interfered with his attempt at serious communication. He was visibly distressed, and I was in shock. From that experience, I learned that there is a time and place for everything. Acting silly when someone was under stress and needed to talk to me wasn't appropriate. This manager taught me a valuable lesson. I realize it's difficult for my friends to imagine, but I am much more serious now — well, when it's absolutely necessary.

Most managers dwell on how to deliver feedback rather than how to receive it. But a crucial lesson in life is the ability to solicit and accept criticism. As effective managers, we need to listen at least as often and as well as we speak.

Feedback can be beneficial, depending on our attitude. I worked with a manager in the 1980s who was so intimidating and close-minded that no one was willing to offer an opinion about anything. One older staff member actually had a heart attack during a particularly stressful confrontation. I stayed up two nights preparing a detailed presentation for this individual, and he skipped to the last slide and started yelling at me. Unfortunately, this senior manager never put down his guard long enough to receive feedback on his behavior. And the company tolerated it. He alienated everyone he knew and seriously hurt business. Projects failed because of his inability to listen to peers, which drove me to leave the company.

We don't have to accept all advice as gospel truth, however. We can receive input with grace and then reflect on it before deciding whether to accept or reject it.

An element of truth often can help us become more effective managers and compassionate human beings.

In challenging times of reduced budgets and rapidly evolving technology, a defensive posture is tempting. However, an inability to respond to new realities can eventually threaten even the most secure job position. It's tough to imagine an enlightened manager who isn't open to change.

Progress rarely comes without suffering. Many of my most valuable lessons in life have been the products of painful experiences. Moving forward means listening to others while putting aside fears and close-mindedness. That's the only way I know to teach us old dogs new tricks.

Sending mixed messages

Ten ways to improve

your communication style

Next to figuring out how to program a DVD player, clearly communicating with others is perhaps the most difficult task confronting managers. The DVD may eventually become a relic of the past, but the need for effective communications is here to stay.

Managers can dramatically improve the health of their relationships by reflecting on their communications style. Some of the barriers to good communication I have experienced — and perpetrated — are:

1. Shooting the messenger. Responding negatively to the bearer of bad news ensures that employees will never speak up again. Try to show appreciation for the courage it took to come forward.

2. Not matching words to actions. People usually believe what they see, not what they hear. Employees respect and enthusiastically support managers who "walk the walk." Are your actions consistent with the directions you have given?

3. Focusing only on yourself. Managers who turn every conversation or meeting into a chance to talk about themselves can suck the energy from a workplace. They send the message that employees aren't important. Focus on others' needs and develop your listening skills.

4. Not keeping an open mind. An honest dialogue implies that both parties are open to altering their points of view. Interrupting is often the sign of a closed mind. Managers who complete employees' sentences might as well work alone.

5. Sending mixed messages. Organizations that send conflicting signals de-motivate their staff. Try communicating a few main objectives and sticking to them. Managers who make everything seem important or routinely switch priorities rarely succeed.

6. Generalizing. Comments such as "you're always late" or "you never return e-mail messages" don't encourage problem-solving. Instead of making others feel inferior, work with your employees to fix problems.

7. Using one-size-fits-all approaches. Rewarding employees for something they don't care about is ineffective. Take the time to understand your employees'

personal and career desires, and tailor rewards accordingly.

8. Resorting to sarcasm and name calling. People rarely respond positively to negative criticism. A tendency toward this kind of behavior is a sure sign of management dysfunction.

9. Asking "what can I get out of you?" Every conversation shouldn't center on what your employees can do for you. What is preventing them from getting their jobs done? Do they understand what is expected of them? Are their needs being met?

10. Saying "not today — I'm too busy." A manager's inability to regularly interact with others can immobilize an organization. Leave your door open and get out of your office. Deal directly with conflicts and obstacles, and keep in mind that projects rarely run smoothly. A manager's job is to work side-by-side with employees, not look down on them from above.

Kick it off right

10 steps for launching a successful project

It is amazing how many managers dive into a new project without taking the time to identify and meet with all the main stakeholders. One of my worst experiences as a young engineer -- back when it practically took a mainframe to play "Dungeons and Dragons" -- was to work for a project manager who didn't know how to provide specific direction. Instead, he expected his staff to intuitively know what was expected.

This lack of communication was a nightmare. I call this "stream of consciousness" management. It's not too bad for stand-up comedy but rarely results in success in the business and government arena.

One way to avoid this type of reactive behavior is to have a well-thought out, proactive project kickoff meeting. It is as important as making sure all the subcontractors understand a building blueprint before they lay the foundation.

The main elements of a successful project team kickoff meeting are:

1. Distributing the agenda beforehand.

2. Beginning and ending on time. Stick to a meeting plan and defer more lengthy digressions to another time.

3. Introducing your project team and major project influencers. Make sure everyone is clear on roles, responsibilities and expectations.

4. Describing the scope and objectives of the project. Don't assume your staff has thoroughly read the statement of work. But make sure you have.

5. Explaining your approach to accomplishing the project including the schedule and critical path. Review the work plan, major milestones and deliverables.

6. Defining success criteria so the team is clear about your client's expectations.

7. Identifying any risks, challenges and project constraints. Take the time to respond to everyone's concerns about the project's success. Don't assume silence is concurrence. Now is the time to encourage open discussion while there is still time to change the plan.

8. Making sure everyone understands the necessary project control and status requirements, including documentation standards and quality reviews. Also, clarify timekeeping and invoicing requirements for other direct charges like travel expenses.

9. Going over the tools, documents and support needed from the client.

10. Recording decisions and action assignments.

A strong beginning will greatly increase the probability of project success and will, I hope, keep you out of the dungeon.

A dash of appreciation

Nothing is more motivating to

a person than feeling appreciated

For several years, I've written about how managers can become more enlightened and supportive of their staff. Although I will continue to cajole and badger you about what you don't do, my wife suggested that I recognize the many things that managers do well. But before I write about the importance of appreciation in the workplace, I will express my appreciation for all of you government and industry managers who:

- Come to work even when you don't feel like it.
- Do more with less and produce inspiring results.
- Work hard to achieve a mission even when no when else is looking.

- Accommodate unfathomable political agendas.
- Support your sometimes less-than-capable senior managers.
- Encourage and assist your sometimes-less-than-capable peers and junior staff.
- Grin and bear it through endless external interviews and audits, with little expectation of positive results.
- Comply with regulations, requirements, submissions and reports that often have little to do with completing your job.
- Try to understand what motivates your industry and government partners.

No offense intended, but not one of the organizations I have worked with has been fully functional. Agencies and companies reflect the strengths and weaknesses of their leaders and have the limitations of other small and large businesses or bureaucracies. Any organization can be criticized.

For some of my career, I felt underappreciated. I had supervisors who treated compliments like rare gems to be seldom distributed. This is unfortunate because feeling unappreciated usually makes people withdraw rather than improve their job performance.

When a manager has a conflict with a peer or employee, often all it takes to open the door to a more positive relationship is for either one of them to express appreciation for something about the other person.

Appreciated people are more likely to reflect on their behavior and change it when necessary. The best appreciation comes from the heart without qualifications.

Many people find it difficult to accept compliments. They respond to praise with, "Oh, I didn't do that much" or, "It wasn't that good." Try owning your accomplishment. You deserve to be appreciated and by accepting appreciation, you make the person expressing it feel good, too.

Showing appreciation is important in all areas of our lives. As my wife likes to remind me, what works at work also works at home. She has been a truly remarkable partner for more than 39 years. (I hope she reads that.) As for all of you, try expressing appreciation. It can and should become habit-forming.

Listen, care and engage

Set clear objectives and
inspire your employees

My favorite time to reflect on past business experiences is the 30-minute ferry ride to downtown Seattle to meet with clients. The gentle swaying of the boat as it navigates Puget Sound summons unfettered thoughts. Some, on rare occasions, are actually meaningful.

I remember how proud I was to participate in the space shuttle project in the early 1980s. That motivation helped me get through some tough work conditions.

Something else that made the experience worthwhile was my immediate supervisor. Bill resembled the Looney Tunes cartoon character Yosemite Sam, with leather cowboy boots, a broad-brimmed hat and a red handlebar moustache. I learned from Bill, one of my best managers, that having the power and authority to make things happen isn't the same as being a leader.

He knew how to set clear objectives, inspire his employees to care about those goals, acquire the necessary resources and then to leave us alone to excel. We followed him because he earned our trust, and not because he carried a big stick.

History books are full of examples of authoritarian leaders. Although such behavior might be appropriate on the battlefield, it leaves a lot to be desired in most companies and government agencies.

Unfortunately, it is still prevalent in technical organizations, where competent specialists assume management responsibilities without leadership capacity or willingness to learn.

Common management philosophy would have us believe that leaders are not born but made. In general, I agree with this. But I also believe some people would be better off remaining on a technical track or in a supporting role. They are no better suited to take on an organizational management position than I am to be a professional athlete. Organizations do themselves a disservice when they only offer a management track as a promotion or salary increase.

True leaders can manifest their power and capability because their followers have the potential for greatness.

Leaders should never become self-satisfied. They should continue to develop as human beings. By remaining students, they can teach instead of preach.

Everyone in an organization deserves respect and is capable of leading by example. Effective managers should care about their employees. Progressive leaders don't hide in their offices, expecting everyone to visit them while they sit on their thrones. Instead, they talk to their peers and employees to engage in meaningful discussions.

As managers, we need to nurture the next generation of capable leaders through our own enlightened behavior.

Don't count your neighbors' wealth

Maintain a balanced perspective between

internal and external job satisfaction

Have you ever sat by while someone less deserving got the promotion you wanted? Or, was put in charge of a highly visible new project even though everyone knows you:

- worked harder
- contributed more and
- really wanted it

There's an old Buddhist saying that goes something like, "a poor man spent night and day counting his neighbor's wealth but gained not even half a coin."

It's difficult sometimes not to compare ourselves with others -- especially if we judge our self-worth only by our job title, financial earnings or professional standing. I not so fondly recall the emotional angst I experienced in my twenties and thirties waiting for another promotion or new assignment only to watch someone else get rewarded. Eventually I realized that my inner happiness was too tied to my external circumstances. There would always be a more prestigious position or a bigger office to play with my emotions.

I had to do some significant self-reflection and attitude adjustment to reduce my attachment to the outer trappings of management. So, while there is definitely nothing inherently wrong with being motivated to get a promotion or more responsibility or a higher salary, I began to take the less visible but important step of being more supportive of my colleagues and also increased my focus on mission success. While my efforts weren't always recognized, I definitely experienced increased work satisfaction. I also discovered it was less judgmental and took less energy to be happy for the good fortune bestowed on my fellow managers.

Unfortunately, not too many organizational cultures foster a more enlightened type of management behavior. Highly competitive performance rankings and an overemphasis on job status can cause exactly the kind of environment that causes individuals to feel shortchanged and underappreciated.

Still, blaming our situation on a dysfunctional organization or biased senior management, even if true, doesn't really help us. An enlightened manager should try to maintain a balanced perspective between internal and external job satisfaction. Being good is more important than being recognized. And, we should extend this behavior to expressing our appreciation to the people who support us. Do they know we value their contribution or have we left them to wallow in jealous misery?

As long as our happiness is circumstantial, we'll probably continue to count our neighbor's money. But, just because our society encourages us to always want more, doesn't mean we can't decide to be happy with what we have.

Final Words

Thank you for reading *The Enlightened Manager.* Additional copies of this book can be purchased at www.amazon.com.

I would be happy to talk to you about your strategic planning, business growth and risk management needs as well as public speaking engagements.

Michael Lisagor

206-780-4202 (PST)

lisagor@celerityworks.com

www.celerityworks.com

Romancing the Buddha (Middleway Press)

By Michael Lisagor

www.romancingthebuddha.com

A 46 minute DVD of *Romancing the Buddha*, a one-man play, is also available at www.amazon.com

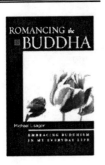

1820044

Made in the USA